PULLMAN CAR
HIAWATHA

A Play in One Act

by

THORNTON WILDER

SAMUEL FRENCH

LONDON
NEW YORK TORONTO SYDNEY HOLLYWOOD

ISBN 978-0-573-02220-3

www.samuelfrench-london.co.uk

www.samuelfrench.com

FOR AMATEUR PRODUCTION ENQUIRIES

UNITED KINGDOM AND WORLD EXCLUDING NORTH AMERICA
plays@SamuelFrench-London.co.uk
020 7255 4302/01

Each title is subject to availability from Samuel French,

depending upon country of performance.

CHARACTERS

THE STAGE MANAGER
. A MAIDEN LADY
A PORTER
AN ENGINEER
ANOTHER ENGINEER
A STOUT AMIABLE WOMAN
A MIDDLE-AGED DOCTOR
PHILIP MILBURY
HARRIET MILBURY
AN INSANE WOMAN
HER NURSE
HER ATTENDANT
GROVERS COMERS, represented by a Grinning Boy
THE FIELD, represented by Somebody in Shirt Sleeves
A TRAMP
PARKERSBURG. OHIO, represented by a Farmer's Wife and Three
    Young People
A WORKMAN
ANOTHER WORKMAN
THE WEATHER, represented by a Mechanic
TEN O'CLOCK   ⎫
ELEVEN O'CLOCK ⎬ represented by
TWELVE O'CLOCK ⎭ Three Beautiful Girls
SATURN
VENUS
JUPITER
THE EARTH
GABRIEL
MICHAEL

PULLMAN CAR *HIAWATHA*

*At the back of the stage is a balcony or bridge or runway lead-
ing out of sight in both directions. Two flights of stairs
descend from it to the stage. There is no further scenery.*

At the rise of the CURTAIN, THE STAGE MANAGER *is
making lines with a piece of chalk on the floor of the stage
by the footlights.*

THE STAGE MANAGER. This is the plan of a pullman
car. Its name is *Hiawatha*, and on December the
twenty-first it is on its way from New York to Chicago.
Here at your left are three compartments. Here is the
aisle, and five lowers. The berths are all full, uppers
and lowers, but for the purposes of this play we are
limiting our interest to the people in the lower berths
on the further side only. The berths are already made
up. It is half-past nine. Most of the passengers are in
bed behind the green curtains. They are dropping
their shoes on to the floor, or wrestling with their
trousers, or wondering whether they dare hide their
valuables in the pillow-slips during the night. All
right! Come on, everybody.

*(The actors enter carrying chairs. Each improvises his
berth by placing two chairs 'facing one another' in his chalk-
marked space. They then sit in one chair, profile to the
audience, and rest their feet on the other. This must do for
lying in bed. The passengers in the compartments do the
same.*

 Reading from L *to* R *we have:*
*Compartment Three: an insane woman with a male atten-
dant and a trained nurse.*
Compartment Two: PHILIP MILBURY, *and*
Compartment One: HARRIET, *his young wife.*
LOWER ONE: *a maiden lady.*
LOWER THREE: *a middle-aged doctor.*

LOWER FIVE: *a stout amiable woman of fifty.*
LOWER SEVEN: *an engineer going to California.*
LOWER NINE: *another engineer.*

*There is a pleasant confusion while these characters
make up their berths. Then* THE STAGE MANAGER *cries:*
All right. We're ready; begin)

LOWER ONE. Porter, be sure and wake me up at
quarter of six.
PORTER. Yes, ma'am.
LOWER ONE. I know I shan't sleep a wink, but I
want to be told when it's quarter of six.
PORTER. Yes, ma'am.
LOWER SEVEN (*putting his head through the curtains*)
Hsst Porter! Hsst! How the hell do you turn on this
other light?
PORTER (*fussing with it*) I'm afraid it's out of order,
sah. You'll have to use the other end.
THE STAGE MANAGER (*falsetto—substituting for some
woman in an upper berth*) May I ask if someone in this
car would be kind enough to lend me some aspirin?
PORTER (*rushing about*) Yes, ma'am.
LOWER NINE (*descending the aisle and falling into
Lower Five*). Sorry, lady, sorry. Made a mistake.
LOWER FIVE (*grumbling*) Never in all my born days!
LOWER ONE (*in a shrill whisper*) Porter! Porter!
PORTER. Yes, ma'am.
LOWER ONE. My hot-water bag's leaking. I guess
you'll have to take it away. I'll have to do without it
tonight. How awful!
LOWER FIVE (*sharply; to the passenger above her*)
Young man, you mind your own business or I'll report
you to the conductor.
THE STAGE MANAGER (*substituting for Upper Five*)
Sorry, ma'am, I didn't mean to upset you. My sus-
penders fell down and I was trying to catch them.
LOWER FIVE. Well, here they are. Now go to sleep.
Everybody seems to be rushing into my berth tonight.
(*She puts her head out*) Porter! Porter! Be a good soul
and bring me a glass of water, will you? I'm parched.

LOWER NINE. Bill! (*No answer*) Bill!
LOWER SEVEN. Ya? What d'y'a want?
LOWER NINE. Slip me one of those magazines, willya?
LOWER SEVEN. Which one d'y'a want?
LOWER NINE. Either one. *Detective Stories.* Either one.
LOWER SEVEN. Aw, Fred. I'm just in the middle of one of 'm in *Detective Stories.*
LOWER NINE. That's all right. I'll take *The Western.* Thanks.
THE STAGE MANAGER (*to the actors*) All right. Sh-sh-sh. That's enough of that. (*To the audience*) Now I want you to hear them thinking.

(*There is a pause and then they all begin a murmuring-swishing noise, very soft. In turn each of them can be heard above the others*)

LOWER FIVE (*the lady of fifty*) Let's see: I've got the doll for the baby. And the slip-on for Marietta. And the fountain-pen for Herbert. And the subscription to *Time* for George . . . (*Her voice subsides into the humming*).
LOWER NINE (*the engineer*) That was the craziest thing I ever did. It's set me back three whole years. I could have saved up thirty thousand dollars by now if I'd only stayed over here. What business had I got to fool with contracts with the goddarned Soviets! Hell, I thought it would be interesting! Interesting, what-the-hell! It's set me back three whole years. I don't know if the company'll even take me back. I'm green, that's all. I just don't grow up.

(*Then*)

LOWER THREE (*the doctor; reading aloud to himself from a medical journal the most hair-raising material, every now and then punctuating his reading with an interrogative*) So?

(*Then*)

LOWER ONE (*the maiden lady*) I know I'll be awake all night. I might just as well make up my mind to do it now. I can't imagine what got hold of that hot-water bag to leak on the train of all places. Well, now I'll lie on my right side and breathe deeply and think of beautiful things and perhaps I can doze off a bit . . .

(*And lastly*)

LOWER SEVEN (*the other engineer*) God! Lilian, if you don't turn out to be what I think you are, I don't know what I'll do. I guess it's bad politics to let a woman know that you're going all the way to California to see her. I'll think up a song-an-dance about a business trip or something. Was I ever as hot-and-bothered about anyone like this before? Well, there was Martha. But that was different. I better try and read or I'll go cuckoo. 'How did you know it was ten o'clock when the visitor left the house?' asked the detective. 'Because at ten o'clock,' answered the girl, 'I always turn out the lights in the conservatory and in the back hall. As I was coming down the stairs I heard the master talking to someone at the front door. I heard him say, "Well, good night, Doctor." ' . . . Gee, I don't feel like reading. I'll just think about Lilian. That yellow hair. Them eyes . . .

(THE STAGE MANAGER *strides towards them with lifted hand, crying 'Hush', and their whispering ceases*)

THE STAGE MANAGER. That'll do. That'll do. Now the compartments.

(*The berths fall into shadow.* PHILIP *is standing at the door connecting his compartment with his wife's*)

PHILIP. Are you all right, angel?
HARRIET. Yes, I don't know what was the matter with me during dinner.
PHILIP. Shall I close the door?
HARRIET. Do see whether you can't put a chair against it that will hold it half-open without banging.
PHILIP. There. Good night, angel. If you can't sleep, call me and we'll sit up and play Russian Bank.

HARRIET. You're thinking of that awful time when we sat up and played every night for a week. But at least I know I shall sleep tonight. The noise of the wheels has become sort of nice and homely. What State are we in?

PHILIP. We're tearing through Ohio. We'll be in Indiana soon.

HARRIET. I know those little towns full of horse blocks.

PHILIP. Well, we reach Chicago very early. I'll call you. Sleep tight.

HARRIET. Sleep tight, my darling.

(PHILIP *returns into his own compartment. In Compartment* THREE, *the* MALE ATTENDANT *tips his chair back against the wall and smokes a cigar. The trained* NURSE *knits a stocking.* THE INSANE WOMAN *leans her forehead against the window-pane, that is, stares into the audience*)

THE INSANE WOMAN (*her words have a dragging, complaining sound, but lack any conviction*) Don't take me there. Don't take me there.

THE NURSE. Wouldn't you like to lie down, dearie?

THE INSANE WOMAN. I want to get off the train. I want to go back to New York.

THE NURSE. Wouldn't you like me to brush your hair again? It's such a nice feeling.

THE INSANE WOMAN (*going to the door*) I want to get off the train. I want to open the door. (*She starts to beat on the door weakly*)

THE NURSE (*taking one of her hands*) Such a noise! You'll wake up all the nice people. Come and I'll tell you a story about the place we're going to.

THE INSANE WOMAN. I don't want to go to that place.

THE NURSE (*her pronunciation of the word 'lovely', her favourite, is appallingly stale and saccharine*) Oh, it's lovely! There are lawns and gardens everywhere. I never saw such a place. Just lovely.

THE INSANE WOMAN (*lying down on her bed*) Are there roses?

THE NURSE. Roses! Red, yellow, white . . . just everywhere.

THE ATTENDANT (*after a pause*) That musta been Cleveland.

THE NURSE. I had a case in Cleveland once for six months. Diabetes.

THE ATTENDANT (*after another pause*) I wisht I had a radio here. Radios are good for them. I had a patient once that had to have the radio going every minute.

THE NURSE. Radios are lovely. My married niece has one. It's always going. It's wonderful.

THE INSANE WOMAN (*half-rising*) I'm not beautiful. I'm not beautiful as she was.

THE NURSE. Oh, I think you're beautiful. Beautiful. Mr Morgan, don't you think Mrs Churchill is beautiful?

THE ATTENDANT. Oh, fine lookin'. Regular movie-star Mrs Churchill.

(THE INSANE WOMAN *looks inquiringly at them and subsides.* HARRIET *groans slightly, and smothers a cough. She gropes about with her hand and finds a bell. The* PORTER *knocks at her door*)

HARRIET (*whispering*) Come in. First please close the door into my husband's room. Softly. Softly.

PORTER (*a plaintive porter*) Yes, ma'am.

HARRIET. Porter, I'm not well. I'm sick. I must see a doctor.

PORTER. Why, ma'am, they ain't no doctor . . .

HARRIET. Yes, when I was coming out from dinner I saw a man in one of these seats on that side reading medical magazines. Go and wake him up.

PORTER (*flabbergasted*) Ma'am, I cain't wake anybody up!

HARRIET. Yes, you can. Porter. Porter. Now don't argue with me. I'm very sick. It's my heart. Wake him up. Tell him it's my heart.

PORTER. Yes, ma'am.

(THE PORTER *goes into the aisle and starts pulling at the shoulder of Lower Three*)

LOWER THREE. Hello. Hello. What is it? Are we there?

(*The* PORTER *mumbles to him*)

I'll be right there. Porter, is it a young woman or an old one?

PORTER. I do'no, sa. I guess she's kinda old, sa, but not so very old.

LOWER THREE. Tell her I'll be there in a minute, and to lie quietly.

PORTER. Yessa.

(*The* PORTER *enters Harriet's compartment. She has turned her head away*)

He'll be here in a minute, ma'am. He says you lie quiet.

(LOWER THREE *stumbles along the aisle, muttering:* 'Damn these shoes')

SOMEONE'S VOICE. Can't we have a little quiet in this car, please?

LOWER NINE (*Fred*) Oh, shut up!

(*The* DOCTOR *passes the* PORTER *into Harriet's compartment. He leans over her, concealing her by his stooping figure*)

LOWER THREE. She's dead, Porter. Is there anyone on the train travelling with her?

PORTER. Yes, sir. Dat's her husband in dere.

LOWER THREE. Idiot! Why didn't you call him? I'll go in and speak to him.

(THE STAGE MANAGER *comes forward*)

THE STAGE MANAGER. All right. So much for the inside of the car. That'll be enough of that for the present. (*He turns to the audience*) Now for its position geographically, meteorologically, astronomically, theologically considered. Pullman car *Hiawatha*, ten minutes of ten, December twenty-first, Nineteen-Thirty. All ready.

(Some figures begin to appear on the balcony)

No, no! It's not time for the Planets yet. Nor the Hours.

(They retire. THE STAGE MANAGER *claps his hands.*
A Grinning Boy in overalls enters from L *behind the berths)*

GROVERS COMERS *(in a foolish voice, as though he were reciting a piece at a Sunday School entertainment)* I represent Grovers Comers, Ohio. Eight hundred and twenty-one souls. 'There's so much good in the worst of us and so much bad in the best of us that it ill behoves any of us to criticize the rest of us.' Robert Louis Stevenson. Thank ya.

*(*GROVERS COMERS *grins and goes out,* R.
Enter from the same direction Somebody in Shirt Sleeves. This is a field)

THE FIELD. I represent a field you are passing between Grovers Comers, Ohio, and Parkersburg, Ohio. In this field there are fifty-one gophers, two hundred and six field-mice, twelve snakes and millions of bugs, insects, ants and spiders—all in their winter sleep. 'What is so rare as a day in June? Then if ever come perfect days.' The vision of Sir Launfal, William Cullen—I mean, James Russell Lowell.

*(*THE FIELD *exits*
A TRAMP *enters)*

THE TRAMP. I just want to tell you that I'm a tramp that's been travelling under the car *Hiawatha*, so I have a right to be in this play. I'm going from Rochester, New York, to Joliet, Illinois. It takes a lot of people to make a world. 'On the road to Mandalay, where the flying fishes play and the sun comes up like thunder, out of China crost the bay.' Frank W. Service. Thank you.

*(*THE TRAMP *exits.*
A GENTLE OLD FARMER'S WIFE *and* THREE YOUNG PEOPLE *enter)*

PARKERSBURG, OHIO. I represent Parkersburg, Ohio. Two thousand six hundred and four souls. I have seen all the dreadful havoc that alcohol has done and I hope no one here will ever touch a drop of the curse of this beautiful country. (*She beats a measure and they all sing unsteadily:* 'Throw out the life-line. Throw out the life-line. Someone is sinking today-ay . . .')

(THE STAGE MANAGER *waves them away tactfully.*
A WORKMAN *enters*)

THE WORKMAN. Ich bin der Arbeiter der hier sein Leben verlor. Bei der Sprengung fur diese Brücke uber die Sie in dem Moment fahren, erschlug mich ein Felsblock. Ich spiele jetzt als Geist in diesem Stuck mit. 'Vor sieben und achtzig Jahren haben unsere Väter auf diesem Continent eine neue Nation hervorgebracht . . .'

THE STAGE MANAGER (*helpfully, to the audience*) I'm sorry; that's in German. He says that he's the ghost of a workman who was killed while they were building the trestle over which the car *Hiawatha* is now passing——

(*The engine whistles again*)

—and he wants to appear in the play. A chunk of rock hit him while they were dynamiting. His motto, you know: Three score and seven years ago our forefathers brought forth upon this continent a new nation dedicated . . . and so on. Thank you, Mr Muller.

(THE WORKMAN *exits.*
Another WORKER *enters*)

THIS Worker. I'm a watchman in a tower near Parkersburg, Ohio. I just want to tell you that I'm not asleep and that the signals are all right for this train. I hope you all have a fine trip. 'If you can keep your head when those about you are losing theirs and blaming it on you.' Rudyard Kipling. Thank you.

(THE WORKER *exits.* THE STAGE MANAGER *comes forward*)

THE STAGE MANAGER. All right. That'll be enough of that. Now the Weather, please.

(*A* MECHANIC *enters*)

THE WEATHER. It is eleven degrees above zero. The wind is north-north-west, velocity, fifty-seven. There is a low field of barometric pressure moving eastward from Saskatchewan towards the eastern coast. To-morrow will be cold with some snow in the Middle Western States and Western New York.

(*The* MECHANIC *exits*)

THE STAGE MANAGER. Now for the Hours, please. (*To the audience*) The Minutes are gossips; the Hours are philosophers; the Years are theologians. The Hours are philosophers except Twelve O'Clock, who is also a theologian. Ready, Ten O'Clock.

(*The* HOURS *are Beautiful Girls dressed like Elihu Vedder's Pleiades. Each carries a great gold Roman numeral. They pass slowly across the balcony at the back, moving from* R *to* L)

What are you doing, Ten O'Clock? Aristotle?
TEN O'CLOCK. No, Plato, Mr Washburn.
THE STAGE MANAGER. Good! 'Are you not rather convinced that he who thus sees Beauty . . .'
TEN O'CLOCK. 'Are you not rather convinced that he who thus sees Beauty as only it can be seen will be specially favoured? And since he is in contact not with images, but with realities . . .'

(TEN O'CLOCK *continues the passage in an inaudible murmur as* ELEVEN O'CLOCK *appears*)

ELEVEN O'CLOCK. What else can I, Epictetus, do, a lame old man, but sing hymns to God? If then I were a nightingale I would do a nightingale's part. If I were a swan I would do a swan's . . .

(ELEVEN O'CLOCK'S *voice, too, subsides to a murmur.* TWELVE O'CLOCK *appears*)

THE STAGE MANAGER. Good! Twelve O'Clock, what have you?

TWELVE O'CLOCK. Saint Augustine and his mother.

THE STAGE MANAGER. 'And we began to say: If in any man the tumult of the flesh were hushed . . .'

TWELVE O'CLOCK. 'And we began to say: If in any man the tumult of the flesh were hushed; hushed the images of earth; of waters and of air . . .'

THE STAGE MANAGER. Faster: 'hushed also the poles of heaven . . .'

TWELVE O'CLOCK. 'Yea were the very soul to be hushed to herself . . .'

THE STAGE MANAGER. A little louder, Miss Foster.

TWELVE O'CLOCK (*a little louder*) 'Hushed all dreams and imagined revelations . . .'

THE STAGE MANAGER (*waving them back*) All right. All right. Now the Planets.

(*The* HOURS *unwind and return to their dressing-rooms* R.

The PLANETS *appear on the balcony. Some of them take their places halfway up the steps. They have no words, but each has a sound. One has a pulsating zinging sound. Another has a thrum. One whistles ascending and descending scales.* SATURN *makes a slow obstinate humming sound on two repeated low notes*)

Louder, Saturn; Venus, higher. Good! Now, Jupiter. Now the Earth. (*He turns back to the beds on the train*) Come on, everybody. This is the Earth's sound.

(*The* TOWNS, *etc., begin to appear. The* PASSENGERS *begin their 'thinking' murmur*)

Come Grovers Comers, Parkersburg, you're in this. Watchman. Tramp. This is the Earth's sound.

(THE STAGE MANAGER *conducts it as the director of an orchestra would. Each of the characters does his motto.* THE INSANE WOMAN *breaks into passionate weeping. She rises and stretches out her arms towards The Stage Manager*)

THE INSANE WOMAN. Use me. Give me something to do. (*She runs stumbling all about the stage*)

(THE STAGE MANAGER *goes to her quickly, whispers in her ear, and leads her back to her guardians. She is unconsoled*)

THE STAGE MANAGER. Now sh-sh! everybody. Enter the Archangels. (*To the audience*) We have now reached the theological position of pullman car *Hiawatha*.

(*The* TOWNS, *the* TRAMP, *etc., have disappeared. The* PLANETS, *off stage, continue a faint music.*
    Two young men in blue serge suits enter along the balcony and descend the stairs at R. *They advance among the beds on the train. As they pass each bed the passenger talks in his sleep.* GABRIEL *points out Bill to* MICHAEL, *who smiles with raised eyebrows. They pause before Lower Five and* MICHAEL *makes the sound of assent that can only be rendered as Nh-Nh. The remarks that the characters make in their sleep are not all intelligible, being lost in the sound of sigh or groan or whisper by which they are conveyed. But we seem to hear:*)

LOWER NINE (*loud*) Some people are slower than others, that's all.

LOWER SEVEN (*Bill*) It's no fun, y'know. I'll try.

LOWER FIVE (*the lady of the Christmas presents; rapidly*) You know best, of course. I'm ready whenever you are. One year's like another.

LOWER ONE. I can teach sewing. I can sew.

(*They approach Harriet's compartment. The* INSANE WOMAN *sits up and speaks to them*)

THE INSANE WOMAN. Me?

(*They shake their heads*)

What possible use can there be in my simply waiting? Well, I'm grateful for anything, I'm grateful for being so much better than I was. Yes. The old story, the terrible story, doesn't haunt me as it used to. A great

load seems to have been taken off my mind. But no
one understands me any more. At last I understand
myself perfectly, but no one else understands a thing
I say. So I must wait?

(*They nod, smiling*)

Well, you know best. (*She adds resignedly and with a
smile that implies complicity*) I'll do whatever is best; but
everyone is so childish, so absurd. They have no logic.
These people are all so mad . . . These people are like
children; they have never suffered.

(The INSANE WOMAN *returns to her bed, and sleeps.
The* ARCHANGELS *stand beside Harriet. The* DOCTOR
has drawn PHILIP *into the next compartment and is talking
to him in earnest whispers.* HARRIET'S *face has been towards the wall; she turns it slightly and speaks towards the
ceiling*)

HARRIET. I wouldn't be happy there. Let me stay
dead down here. I belong here. I shall be perfectly
happy to roam about my house and be near Philip.
You know I wouldn't be happy there.

(GABRIEL *leans over and whispers into her ear. After a
short pause* HARRIET *bursts into fierce tears*)

I'm ashamed to come with you. I haven't done anything, I haven't done anything with my life. Worse
than that! Worse than that, I was angry and sullen.
I never realized anything. Oh, I don't dare go a step
in such a place.

(*They whisper to her again*)

But it's not possible to forgive such things. I don't
want to be forgiven so easily. I want to be punished
for it all. I won't stir until I've been punished a long,
long time. I want to be freed of all that—by punish-
ment. I want to be all new.

(*They whisper to her.* HARRIET *puts her feet slowly on
the ground*)

But no one else could be punished for me. I'm willing to face it all myself. I don't ask anyone to be punished for me.

(*They whisper to her again.* HARRIET *sits long and brokenly, looking at her shoes and thinking it over*)

It wasn't fair. I'd have been willing to suffer for it myself—if I could have endured such a mountain. (*She smiles ruefully through her tears*) Oh, I'm ashamed. I'm just a stupid and you know it. But then, what wonderful things must be beginning now. You really want me? You really want me?

(*They start leading her down the aisle of the car*)

Let's take the whole train. There are some lovely faces on the train. Can't we all come? You'll never find anyone better than Philip. Please, please, let's all go.

(*They reach the steps. The* ARCHANGELS *interlock their arms as a support for* HARRIET *as she leans heavily on them, taking the steps slowly. Her words are half-singing and half-babbling*)

But look how tremendously high and far it is. I have a weak heart. I'm not supposed to climb stairs. 'I do not ask to see the distant scene. One step enough for me.' It's like Switzerland. My tongue keeps saying things, I can't control it. Do let me stop a minute. I want to say good-bye. (*She turns in their arms*) Just a minute, I want to cry on your shoulder. (*She leans her forehead against Gabriel's shoulder and laughs long and softly*) Good-bye, Philip. I begged him not to marry me, but he would. He believed in me, just as you do. I just hoped. Good-bye, One-three-one-two Ridgewood Avenue, Oakesbury. I hope I remember all its steps and doors and wallpapers for ever. Good-bye, Emerson Grammar School on the corner of Forbush Avenue and Wherry Street. Good-bye, Miss Walker and Miss Cramer who taught me English, and Miss Matthewson who taught me Biology. Good-bye, First Congregational Church on the corner of Meyerson

Avenue and Sixth Street, and Dr McReady and Mrs
McReady and Julia. Good-bye, papa and mama——
(*She turns*) Now, I'm tired of saying good-bye. Why I
never used to talk like this. I was so homely I never
used to have the courage to talk. Until Philip came. I
see now. I see now. I understand everything now.

(THE STAGE MANAGER *comes forward*)

THE STAGE MANAGER (*to the actors*) All right. All
right. Now we'll have the whole world together,
please. The whole solar system, please.

(*The complete cast begins to appear at the edges of the
stage.* THE STAGE MANAGER *claps his hands*)

The whole solar system, please. Where's the Tramp?

(THE STAGE MANAGER *gives two raps on the floor like
the conductor of an orchestra attracting the attention of his
forces, and slowly lifts his hand. The human beings murmur their thoughts; the* HOURS *discourse;* PLANETS *chant
or thrum.* HARRIET'S *voice finally rises above them all,
saying:*)

HARRIET. 'I was not ever thus, nor pray'd that
Thou
Shouldst lead me on; and spite of fears,
Pride ruled my will: remember not past years.'

THE STAGE MANAGER (*waving them away*) Now
we're at Englewood Station, South Chicago. See the
University's towers over there: the best of them all.

LOWER ONE (*the spinster*) Porter, you promised to
call me at a quarter of six.

THE PORTER. Sorry, ma'am, but it's been an awful
night on this car. A lady's been terrible sick.

LOWER ONE. Oh!— is she better?

THE PORTER. No'm. She ain't one jot better.

LOWER FIVE. Young man, take your foot out of my
face.

THE STAGE MANAGER (*again substituting for Upper
Five*) Sorry, lady, I slipped.

LOWER FIVE (*grumbling, not unamiably*) I declare this
trip's been one long series of insults.

THE STAGE MANAGER. Just one minute, ma'am, I'll be down and out of your way.

LOWER FIVE. Haven't you got anybody to darn your socks for you? You ought to be ashamed to go around that way.

THE STAGE MANAGER. Sorry, lady.

LOWER FIVE. You're too stuck up to get married. That's the trouble with you.

LOWER NINE. Bill! Bill!

LOWER SEVEN. Ye'? What d'y'a want?

LOWER NINE. Bill, how much d'y'a give the porter on a train like this? I've been outa the country so long . . .

LOWER SEVEN. Hell, Fred! I don't know myself.

THE PORTER. Chicago. Chicago. All out. This train don't go no further.

(*The* PASSENGERS *jostle their way out, and an army of old women with mops and pails enter and prepare to clean up the car*)

Lightning Source UK Ltd.
Milton Keynes UK
UKHW020014120422
401412UK00006B/581